MIXED MESSAGES

Edited by

Rachael Radford

First published in Great Britain in 2002 by
ANCHOR BOOKS
Remus House,
Coltsfoot Drive,
Peterborough, PE2 9JX
Telephone (01733) 898102

HB ISBN 1 84418 058 1
SB ISBN 1 84418 059 X

FOREWORD

Anchor Books is a small press, established in 1992, with the aim of promoting readable poetry to as wide an audience as possible.

We hope to establish an outlet for writers of poetry who may have struggled to see their work in print.

The poems presented here have been selected from many entries, and as always editing proved to be a difficult task.

I trust this selection will delight and please the authors and all those who enjoy reading poetry.

Rachael Radford
Editor

CONTENTS

Hillsborough

How I vividly still remember
The first time I saw Spurs play
Wimbledon the opponents at Plough Lane
The Hillsborough tragedy was the day.

I remember climbing the perimeter fence
Surrounded by children, men and wives
As I watched it was hard to believe
That in Sheffield fans lost their lives.

That day bought life into perspective
So very difficult to comprehend
How in one match many fans
Came to a tragic end.

John Lee

KATE'S DILEMMA

Kate was extremely precise. She liked to have everything nice!
She pursued all her sweeping and rigid housekeeping
With vigour approaching a vice.

One morning a call on the phone made her stifle an agonised groan.
She wasn't quite dressed and she'd be sorely stressed
To get the house fit to be shown.

She swept up a handful of dirt and put on a very full skirt.
Expecting the vicar she had to be quicker.
He'd be there very soon, and alert!

The flowers? She could see a dead rose.
If it spoils the arrangement it goes
She raced for the door and she'd closed it before
She knew it was trapping her clothes.

Her skirt was caught fast in the lock! She very near fainted from shock.
'What a thing to have happened to me for a Yale only opens by key
And it's firm as a primeval rock.'

The moment was fraught, she knew she was caught.
She must open the door that was certainly sure
But the skirt wouldn't move however she fought.

'The vicar can't find me still here, that is abundantly clear;
So the skirt must be shed. Pull it over my head
I can run round the back without fear

I can open the door from inside and it needn't be pushed very wide'
She blanched as she looked at her knickers,
Not garments for welcoming vicars.
Next moment she'd gladly have died.

She'd opened the door just a crack and was horribly taken aback
For the vicar was there with a scandalised air
At the sight of her serious lack.

He gulped! Then he managed to say, 'Dear lady, I really can't stay.
Your condition is such that I can't help you much.
I'll just go off quietly and pray.'

Flora Hughes

The Sun Today

The sun today is shining bright,
And my spirits are riding high,
Fears and troubles in corners are hiding
They won't venture out with the sun in the sky.

A wearisome yesterday all dull and dark
Heralded woe, fear and anxiety are about
Rain in the wind, cold in the air,
Misery prevails without any doubt.

Again the sun is shining bright,
Birds are singing wild and free,
Joy and happiness are born anew
The world is wonderful again, for thee and me.

Margt C Leighton

Think Of Me

Think of me in days and dreams.
Even in sleep, under soft moonbeams.
Think of me while I am gone,
I'm not far, I won't be long.
If you miss me, just close your eyes
And when you do the sun will shine.

L Gill

The Way Forward

Yet another dreary night,
sat here, in my lonely room.
Looking through my window,
at the night-time's eerie gloom.

Since she's been gone,
there's nothing, I can see,
but emptiness all around.
She never cared, about me.

Perhaps tomorrow, I may go out,
and find a new romance.
Someone who really cares,
there's got to be a chance.

Tomorrow, I could be sat here,
holding someone new.
Looking, deep into her eyes,
and whispering, 'I love you'.

That's it, I am going out to find,
a girl that's right for me.
Someone, who is lonely too,
I wonder who she could be?

Edward Elwell

For Alys

(My daughter Alys, now aged seven,
was diagnosed as being autistic three years ago)

What will you do when you're grown up kid?
Vulnerable, beautiful child of mine.
How will you cope with the ways of the world
When I'm no longer there, Love, to keep you in line?

What will you do when you grow up kid?
Will you survive in this world on your own?
Will you find love, someone who understands
Or be destined to live out your life all alone?

What will you be when you grow up kid?
You're bright; you can hold your head up with pride!
You're free to achieve what you want to achieve
Unless they are blind to the real you, inside.

Whatever you do when you grow up kid,
Make sure they don't use you and treat you like dirt.
Your innocence, Love, is a wonderful thing
But it lays you wide open to heartbreak and hurt.

What will you do when you're grown-up kid?
It's a question I'm asking myself every day
For without us to guide you and care for your needs
The ignorants out there may lock you away.

What will happen to you when you're grown up kid?
A fear that I have of the haunting unknown
Makes me want to protect you from reality,
And hope I'm still there for you, when you are grown.

L Foster

Life Of A Sandwich

I started off as a piece of plain, white bread
With crusty, brown bits at my sides, feet and head
Then someone took me out of the wrapper, where I was happy to be
Yes, they'd decided it was to be a sandwich for their tea.

A cold, silver piece of metal, known as a knife
Was thrust over me, I feared dreadfully for my life
But they'd managed to soothe my cuts, 'Thank God' I utter
For over me now was a coating of butter.

I heard them open cupboards and the fridge door
The spread wasn't the only thing, there was going to be more.
A packet was prized apart, a bit of light relief really,
I thought it was to be jam
Then slapped against me, were a couple of slices of ham.

More torture followed, with lettuce, cucumber, tomato and cheese
When was it all going to end? 'Somebody help me please!'
Another rustling of a packet ensued, I could hear my pal scream
As he was planted atop it all, above the salad cream.

A plate was what we were placed on as we're cut into two
This was it, the end, what could we possibly do?
Then came our fate, the final crunch
As we were devoured in a mighty big munch!

Margo Baxter

SEASIDE DAYS

When seas and skies are summer blue the cottonwool clouds so white
To get down to the seaside seems always to be right
To watch the yachts go sailing by bobbing along the seas
Their coloured sails all straining to catch any passing breeze
To sit, to look, to ponder, to read, maybe to dream
Your worries seem to fade away just like a puff of steam.

A walk amid the rockpools to seek a crab or shrimp
They dart around so swiftly, you could miss them should you blink
You come across some seaweed as it wavers to and fro
You wander at the molluscs clinging rocks they won't let go
Maybe you find a starfish, a jellyfish or two
All living things in limbo waiting tides that ebb and flow.

A dabble in a little surf as you stroll along the shore
Could anything be so blissful, you could not ask for anymore,
You hope to see a fish jump, a dolphin leap at play
Perhaps even doing somersaults way out into the bay.

To listen to the seagulls as they call and dip and swirl
The children building castles together, boy or girl,
They gather many pebbles, some shells, maybe a feather too
To decorate their handiwork their parents to laud and view.

The movement of the wavelets as they break along the sands
The little ones so joyful as they jump over holding hands,
Some youngsters playing cricket with a tennis ball and sticks
The older ones a football match as they run and take their kicks.

A distant sound of laughter, somebody strumming tunes
The drifting wood has been gathered, a fire lit amid the dunes,
They sit and cook and chatter so carefree, just so gay
How lovely it is to see them enjoying their summer day.

Marjorie Leyshon

HAWAII

It was Christmastime, a visit I made
    To these lovely isles, in the Pacific they lay.
Flying the heights, one could hardly believe,
    The miles we were covering with such speed.
Fast as we flew it seemed unreal.
    That in a few hours time, the sun we would feel.
Dressed as we started for frost and snow
    Now we could forget it, and meet the sun gold
At last we descended to a sight so rich
    The ocean mixed with such shades of blue.
The sand and the palm trees, with the sun shining through
    The people dressed gaily wandering around
Everyone there, relaxed, friendly and gay
    To enjoy the perfection of where these isles lay
And to renew health and rigour, during their stay.
    The evenings too, a sight to behold
The lights, the music and the people around
    Dressed in a way only these isles could display.
Flying away from these bright sunny isles
    Our feelings as light as the air all around
And yet as we landed back to the ground
    There to greet us was deep snow all around
Although far away in time and miles
    Will I ever forget how happy our smiles
To think and remember for many a day
    Those Pacific islands, so far away.

T J Everett

SOMEBODY

Somebody's hidden my best blue socks
And made a mess in my pencil box
And lost my favourite teddy bear
And squirted toothpaste all over my hair
And given my pen to a boy at school
And left my lunch at the swimming pool
And written my name on my bedroom door
And scattered my clothes all over the floor
And set my little pet spider free.
Oh!
I
Think
That
Somebody
Might
Be
Me!

Maureen Sponar

Deep Inside

I look at you and see a whole lot more
What do you see when you look at me.
I've shown you the way, I've shown you the door
Don't be afraid of me, open up and let me see.

I'll fill that empty, lonely space
I'll make you exhale and learn to breathe
Loneliness will have no trace
I am all you need.

If you want I'll be your private detective
I can read the signals, I'll find the clues
All of me works, nothing is defective
Think about it, don't be confused.

Your confidence may be low
But the feelings you have can't be denied.
It's time that you let them grow
And show me what is . . . *deep inside.*

Nadine Beckford

Flaming June

Flaming June has come at last,
And we'll all be glad when it's flaming well past!
The skies are grey, the rain pours down.
Even the sparrows are wearing a frown.
The tom tits ruffle their feathers, all wet,
And sit in the apple tree's boughs, and fret.
The blackbirds trill, but look so glum;
They seem to be saying 'This is rum
Weather we are having for the month of June.
We hope the sun will come out soon
Or our babies, each as they leave the nest,
Will have to be fitted with a waterproof vest'.
The trees in the garden drip, drip, drip
And the grass is so wet that we nearly slip
When we venture out to look at the sky
To see if the clouds are passing by,
Or if the rain is here to stay,
Feeding the clover but spoiling the hay.
The roses look bedraggled and sad,
And the length of the grass makes Father mad.
The mower stands alone, unused,
And all his prize blooms are getting bruised.
We really feel that we've had enough
Of clouds and rain and all that stuff.
A dose of sunshine is now a must
Before we all go down with terminal rust.

Frances Marie Cecelia Harvey

Understanding

A man stood before me with a cheery grin
I felt so safe, I welcomed him in
There was something about his warm-hearted smile
That deep in my heart - I felt no guile
His presence was warm, an instant rapport
The trust was real - I felt so sure
His huge arms held me in a loving embrace
His soft eyes smiled as he gazed at my face.

We sat and laughed as the years rolled away
'Til we came to the part where I needed to say
'I have something to tell you and I don't know how
Your reaction to it will affect us now.'
I silently asked the presence within
To give me the truth and courage to win
Over the shadow that haunted my past
Truth took my hand with a grip so fast
And a love so strong that I felt no fear
With the silent man that sat so near.

Suddenly, he moved in a different way
My heart missed a beat - is he going to stay
Or walk away as others have done
Before him? Oh, is it all undone?
Love whispered to me in my inner ear
Now, you know, little one, you have nothing to fear
When you tell the truth and learn to forgive
That is the moment you start to live
And grow to be a person so whole
That resides in your being, it is the soul
Imprisoned no more by the cage of the past
A bird that soars high, pure freedom at last.

The man stroked my hand with a loving touch
And a smile so warm that said so much
It is over now, the past so dark
I felt so glad at his kind remark
Now I know - who knocked at the door
It was truth, joy and peace - a love so sure
His farewell words - 'You are never alone'
Was divine love speaking - I'd finally come home.

Gina Bowman

NEGATIVE THOUGHT

(For Kim)

Some people are quite vain
of their photographs they will complain
but the camera will never lie
for it does not have a human eye.

It will photograph you as you are
we can't all be the material of a movie star
as you sit there and proudly pose
all your faults it will expose
you can always try and blame the light
if your snapshot does not turn out right

Maybe a shadow gives the impression of more hair
but come on, honestly be fair
do you really wish vanity was your middle name
even if it was the shot would still turn out the same
so forget about that holiday photo
of that ID badge you wear
it's the real you that people deal with
show them personality and flair.

Chris Black

Snake

What creature is most like me, some people say a snake
Because I'm always cold and thin just like a rake

Upon thinking about it further, some good points I have found
I think being a snake would suit me down to the ground

I could curl up by a radiator and keep myself so warm
I wouldn't show my fangs at all, unless someone wished me harm

Clothes would be no problem, I'd be neat as a new pin
When I got too big for it I'd simply shed my skin

To show a marvellous patterned, sleek and slender form
Not as I feel right now all dowdy and forlorn

I'd be in such good company, with famous snakes of the past
The symbol of life in medicine and Cleopatra's asp

So though you may shake and shiver and maybe want to flee
Just stop a while and ponder, hissss . . . it could be me.

Sandra Skelton

An Embrace

A child stumbles and grazes his knee;
Following the shock the tears run free.
Mum close at hand rushes to console;
Words of comfort and a hug her goal.

The wanderer returns from his distant travel
With a desire to find an audience his itinerary to unravel.
First however the greetings must take their place
So that his return is celebrated with a warming embrace.

Lovers part to follow life's inexorable routine,
Meeting again to re-engage in the previous scene.
Happily reunited, though only hours apart,
A hug and a kiss are but just the start.

Bodily contact in the form of an embrace
Is an essential part of the culture of the human race.
Nothing comforts or warms more than a pleasurable squeeze
And often leaves us with the desire - more please!

Allen Jessop

Sally And Susan

When I enter the shed the guineas come running
Sally so quiet, Susan so funny
Sally so small with her long silky hair
Susan so fat, cuddly and fair
Susan will come when she hears your voice
She'll nuzzle your hand for a tit-bit of choice
Sally is shy and stays near her nest
So Susan takes her a bit of the best.
We laugh when we see how Susan takes charge
Managing Sally so life is not hard
They cuddle together when danger they fear
Under two little bundles two heads disappear.

Joan Patrickson

Blair's Lament

(Written some weeks before the General Election of June 2001)

The winds of change blew through this land just four short years ago
When the voters kicked the Tories out, and told them where to go.
They didn't trust the boom and bust, and were fed up to the teeth
With Howard and Hurd and Heseltine, John Major and Ted Heath.

So I was now in charge of things installed in Number Ten,
Surrounded by my acolytes, all mean ambitious men.
But in a while my well-known smile grew lustreless and pale,
I'd discovered that this Premier job is not all cakes and ale.

We'd put our trust in Mandelson, a devious sort of chap,
But he'd steered our ship to victory and put us on the map
Yet you somehow had the feeling, fight against it how you will,
Though he'd one hand on the tiller, he'd the other in the till.

Gordon Brown went off to town on the 8.21
To try to forge, with Eddie George, a scheme to work upon
The fixing of our interest rates, and whether this should be
The Bank of England's privilege, or left to Brown and me.
Some argued this, some wanted that, it was a right old wrangle,
As all of the alternatives were viewed from every angle.
When I could get a word in I sternly pointed out,
'This must be settled quickly cos the Footsie's up the spout.'

Mo Mowlem went to Ireland though she didn't like it much
But we thought we'd woo the Irish with a woman's gentle touch.
Now the trouble with the Irish is, and never you forget it
They really don't know what they want, but will fight us all to get it.

We had to choose a master for the Foreign Office pack,
This used to be a real grandee, like dear old Supermac.
We looked at the possibles - there really weren't enough.
We'd only chaps like Prescott left, and they're not up to snuff.
Now we've never had a cabinet without a Foreign Sec.
I know that's right because last night we'd told Jack Straw to check.
So the barrel was rolled out again for just one final look,
And there, right at the bottom, was little Robin Cook.

Now I'd like to tell you something, but it's strictly *entre nous*
And *you* have got my word for it, it's absolutely true,
The members of my cabinet don't realise that work
Is something that they have to do, their job's not just a perk.
They think because they're ministers their working days are over
And *they* can swan around the place, like pampered pigs in clover.

With their chauffeurs and their bodyguards and all their other flunkeys,
And *for* pro bonopublico they couldn't give a monkey's.
Due to their incompetence the Party's in a mess.
And you should see the headlines we are getting in the press.
'New Labour's dead' - 'They're in the Red', they're
there in all the papers,
Which brings on my dyspepsia - and Mrs Beckett's vapours.

But I am not responsible for all these ills we've got,
It's my lazy bunch of ministers, I'd like to sack the lot.
I didn't start this foot and mouth - I didn't build the Dome
I didn't tell these immigrants they've got a home from home.
Because of what I've told you I find it hard to see
Why everyone I speak to is so hopping mad at me.

Walter Greenwood

Old Sam

I'm sorry I've forgotten your name
I'm sure it's my age that's to blame.
The only reason I know who I am
Is that folks keep calling me Sam.

Sam Spruce

THE RIVER OF LIFE

From a crack in the earth, a clear spring leapt forth,
this expulsion being the moment of birth
of a river, which was first a stream
of shallow mineral water of modest mien.

The clear water bubbled and swiftly ran
amongst stones and heather and then,
it cut its way both deep and wide,
creating numerous places for creatures to hide.

I stood on the bank by the waters so clear,
amazed to see grey crayfish and trout so near.
They matched the pebbles amidst weeds so green.
The crayfish remained, while the trout swam upstream.

The water grew languid, meandering through pasture,
then gained momentum, going faster and faster.
It rushed over rocks and then with a sigh,
hurtled downwards, launching plumes of spray to the sky.

Our life's like a river if we but knew,
wandering here and there, wondering what to do.
Then we gain momentum and rush along,
doing too many things, and then we are gone.

Suzanna Wilson

Laugh And The Whole World Laughs With You

You only live once on this Earth,
You are born, you live and you die,
Sometimes you have worries, sometimes you are happy.
Sometimes you cry.

Life is a struggle for everyone,
Whether you are rich or poor,
If you are not happy,
Life is a bore.

If someone makes you laugh,
You feel better inside,
Time and tide wait for no one,
If you are unhappy, in someone confide.

When your life is going well,
Be thankful but things can go wrong,
If you are suffering,
Don't give in, stay strong.

Take each day as it comes,
Try to have a laugh,
Talk with friendly, cheerful people,
Join in, stay in their path.

Assuming can be harmful,
Don't live that way,
Think health and happiness,
Each and every day.

Don't harm anyone,
Do unto others as thou would have done unto you,
If you are in love,
Be honest, have fun too.

Whatever your goal,
Try to enjoy your life,
Have a really good laugh,
Deal with any trouble or strife.

John Lewis

Cloud-Like Blankets

Do you grieve for us
Like we grieve for you?
Do you share our tear
Because we've shed a few?
Do you comfort our every fall?
With cloud-like blankets
Your loving shawl.
One smile
Saying you understand
Reaching out your soften hand
Could catch me
Ease my anxiety
Instil my heart to face society.
Tear tasting raindrops
Rest upon pampered rose bud petals
My unconscious mind
Nauseously nests on a bed of nettles
Beer stained breath barely breathing now
Curtain fall imminent
Preparing to make my bow
Disconcerting memories flare up a fright
Rainbow expressions
In the dead of the night
Counting each moment
On my imaginary clock
Praying to God
For my torment to stop.
Cloud-like blanket surrender my fall
Content with my goodnight call.

Peter Wilde

CHRISTMAS DAY

Christmas morning begins to dawn,
Sleepy eyes, a great big yawn.
Down the stairs, children creep,
The rest of the house, still asleep.

Looks of excitement, shouts of glee,
Shiny packages displayed under the tree.
Lots of laughter, squeals of delight,
Ripping off paper so colourful and bright.

Time for the turkey, trimmings too,
Grandma's best crockery, still looking new.
After dinner Grandad snores,
In the kitchen, washing and chores.

An afternoon stroll, a breath of fresh air,
Grandad left behind, still asleep in his chair.
Walk by the river with its rushing flow,
Leaving footprints in the newly laid snow.

In the evening, stories are told,
Outside snow falls, crisp and bold.
For sleepy heads, it's now bedtime,
Through the half-lit window, twinkling stars shine.

Ruth Goodwin

TRACEY BEAKER

Tracey Beaker,
She was quite a speaker,
She never ever stopped,
That was Tracey Beaker.

Tracey Beaker,
She was so happy,
She would go round and say, ‘You happy chappie?’
She was so happy,
That was Tracey Beaker.

Tracey Beaker,
She was upset,
She started to cry and her tears met,
With her lips and she laughed
And said, ‘That tastes funny, Mummy,’
That was Tracey Beaker.

Gemma Smith

SPIDER'S WEB

I watched a spider weave its web
From tiny little bits of silver thread
It grew into a masterpiece.

In awe I saw it catch a fly
And while I watched it slowly die
It became wrapped up like a present.

The spider stored his meal away
To be eaten on another day
When it hungered for a treat.

It ran out to repair a rip
That the fly had made at the end of its trip
And the spider's new home had been broken.

Fascinated I continued to watch
As it darted out each time to catch
Its dinner, lunch or supper.

Every time the web vibrated
The spider appeared and deliberated
Over which meal this one would become.

Raindrops now falling from the overhead cloud
The spider checks the web; he's very house proud
And finds the web now dripping with crystal jewels.

The rain has stopped, the sun has appeared
And to the web I found I've neared
To see the amazing light display.

What a perfect hour I've just spent
Watching the spider become content
And seeing the delights of nature unfolding.

Joanne Hale

Loss Of Dignity

Hold onto your wig, it could blow away,
The forecast says high winds today.
People see, but do not care,
You always wanted long blonde hair.
The wind cares less, it grows so strong,
That lamp post holds your wig, but not for long.
Along the street it merrily goes,
Across the road, as the traffic flows.
How could the wind be cruel like that?
It serves you right, you should have worn a hat.
Of course you'll have some explaining to do,
Because no one knew you were bald,
The only one perhaps was you.

James Ayrey

In My Head . . .

In it there are half-written songs,
Padded bras, g-strings and thongs.
There are potato skins and bits of fluff,
Shampoo, conditioner and dandruff.
In my head are little babies, yes, nos and lots of maybes.
My cool mates are in my head, and me wishing I was in bed.
In my head is a light bulb, and a UFO that revolves.
In it's a long black drain,
And an enormous pea-sized brain.
There are Bertie Bott's every flavour beans,
And Draco Malfoy, he's so mean.
There's half- finished dictionaries, of new come about words,
There's dudes and dorks, geeks and nerds.
There are paper clips and pins, black liners for bins,
There is an entirely new flower,
Never felt before power,
A new thought - of a flower bed,
A thought of life, living and dead.
There are tulip heads, and daisy roots,
Bright purple, flower covered boots.
But away from the noisy, crowded parts of my head,
Away from the thoughts that never leave bed,
There are unearthly, beautiful things,
The amazing sound as the angel sings.
There sits a child, alone in the dark,
With on hands and feet, a nail-like mark.
When you tread on snow, that crunching sound,
Just knowing you have love all around.
All the feelings, before, inside,
These are the things, I unintentionally hide . . .

Katherine Jones (12)

Empty Chairs At Xmas Breakfast 1943

Charlie said
I could have his eggs and bacon,
Because he's dead.
They went down like a fiery beacon
On the final dog-leg to Berlin,
Flames illuminating every straining 'Merlin',
Until the lethal boom
That heralded their doom.
Then a golden rain
Like some 5th November treat,
A funeral pyre at 15,000 feet.
So, seven empty chairs at breakfast
On that Christmas day.
Fourteen forks and knives
Representing terminated, snuffed-out lives,
To be gathered and reshone,
In memory of the seven-man crew
Of a sturdy 'Lanc',
One more bomber, gone!

John Martin

Love

Hatred keeps a man alive
On hatred certain people thrive
Just because love favours others
They withdraw into their covers
And like the ignorant snake
Bring danger and death in their wake
If such a man spreads his poisonous fangs
To trap you, don't despise him
Don't ignore him
Treat him as your unlucky friend
For love reaches limits
Hatred never does.

Pat Ivory

The Advert

'Pretty girl would like to meet
Handsome man who's tall and neat.
Crisp curly hair and eyes of brown,
One who never wears a frown'.

'Oh!' thinks I, 'that sounds like me,
I'll write as soon as can be.'
So quick as a flash I took a pen
And answered the ad with where and when.

I mentioned a pub for a drink and a bite
I said 'The Unicorn', that's white.
Thursday next I thought would do . . .
By then I'd have quid or two.

Came the day the sun shone bright
I sang a song . . . my heart was light.
Then what I saw made my poor head spin . . .
A huge red spot upon my chin!

I sat in the pub with heavy heart,
She's sure to come . . . all dolled up smart.
I bought myself a pint of beer
To give myself a bit of cheer.

Then she came . . . she sidled in
A huge red spot upon her chin.
I saw at once she was my mate
The ad I saw just sealed our fate.

So here we are ten years along
And, thank the Lord, our spots have gone.
But then today our son came in
A huge red spot upon his chin.

I smiled at her . . . she smiled at me
Cos we're just as happy as can be.

Audrey Chester

TED

He sits there in the corner with his head upon his chest,
And listens to the clocks tick, while all around him are at rest.
He feels so very lonely and he's frightened of the dark,
He tries to remember the happy days, when he was taken to the park,
With all his friends around him, all wanting him to play,
And then he'd sleep in someone's bed and dream of the happy day.
But now he's old and tired and losing all his hair,
But I still love him just as much, my dear old Teddy Bear!

Joyce M Woods

Squeak

Squeak
My beautiful tortoiseshell and white guinea pig
With a sweet, twitchy nose and brown eyes big
Four cute tiny paws
Each with three or four claws
Why did you have to go away?

Squeak
You were quiet and gentle
When excited be mental
For food you'd never dash
Never bite or be rash
Why did you have to go away?

Squeak
I remember the time you escaped out your run
Into the bush like the shot of a gun
And when you leapt into a bag of hay
Luckily you were okay
Why did you have to go away?

Squeak
Why did you have to go?
There is still something I want you to know
Whatever happens, whatever I do
I will always remember you
Precious memories of you I'll cart
'Cause you'll always have a place in my heart
You, nobody can replace
I miss you with your cute, cheeky face
I love you
Why did you have to go away?

Jessica Stafford (12)

A Special Friend

Father God, it's good to know
You are my special friend.
From the beginning of the day
Until the very end.
There to listen, comfort, knowing you are near
Really then, there is no need to fear.
Thank you for the good that comes my way
It's great knowing, by me you stay.
For my prayer requests I have made today
Also how you resolve them in your special way.
For the wrong in our troublesome world
Which must break your heart,
If only we had listened to you from the start.
I pray that love will overcome
That peace may reign in the hearts of everyone.
Perhaps we should all begin to care
To look around and be prepared to share.
I thank you for creation and the wonder at your hand
All this in the beginning was in your special plan.
I pray for the elderly, sick and lonely
Those less fortunate in your sight,
That you will especially bless them this night.
A loving touch, a caring smile
Perhaps to linger for a while.
For the very young I pray
Into their hearts you will stay.
Now as I close my eyes tonight
Of you I never will lose sight.

Aves Swanson

Memories Of My Dad

I sit on my dad's lap
Together we take a nap
My dad is very funny
He gives me pocket money
He taught me how to skate
Won't let me stay out late
He will play games with me
And take me to the sea
He buys me sweets
And gives me lots of treats
His legs and arms are hairy
He calls me his Little Fairy
He tickles my tummy
He lives with me and Mummy
And when he gets his pay
He takes us on holiday
When we go to the coast
Is what I like most
Playing on the beaches
Splashing me in the sea 'til I scream
Buying me lots of ice cream
    My dad is great
    He is my best mate
    He takes me to the zoo
    I hope your dad does too
    In my best dress I give him a twirl
    I really am my daddy's girl.

Janet Parker

A Cup Of Tea

When I moved in the curtains twitched
Along the road the noses itched
To catch a glimpse of what I had
I thought, these neighbours must be sad.

Unloading done, van gone away
I looked at all the disarray
No cups or kettle could I find
I thought I'd go out of my mind.

I heard the bell of my front door
A tray was lying on the floor
Cakes and sandwiches with meat
And a pot of tea - oh, what a treat.

I sat down to enjoy this feast
And wondered just which nosy beast
Had been so kind to take the trouble
To welcome me in all this hubble.

Next morning the bell rang again
And there stood neighbours, nine or ten
They all were smiling, holding things
Like home-made jam and plants and tins.

'We didn't think we should intrude
But we wanted to help anyway we could
It's nice round here I'm sure you'll find'
I almost wept - they were so kind.

I've settled in to this new place
I've made a friend of every face
That pot of tea just broke the ice
They aren't nosy, they're just nice.

F Macdonald

My Memories . . .

My memories will carry me
As the years go slowly by,
Of the 'good old days' when life was fair,
You were young and so was I.

Happy days, most of the time,
A few sad, to balance our life.
Loved ones, family and friends,
Who helped out in times of strife.

Walking round the hospital grounds,
We stroll hand in hand, side by side.
We sit on a bench and I talk to you,
Of time when we laughed till we cried.

My memories will carry me
Though yours seem to have abandoned you.
I will reminisce for both of us,
Till the time you remember too.

Polly Davies

VERY IMPORTANT MAN AND WOMAN

(Written during my second term as an
Oxfordshire County Councillor)

I love my father very much,
He is a gentleman.
He never gets flustered or unnerved, no matter what goes on,
He is a very handsome man.

Sometimes many people say to me
With your large eyes and high cheekbones
You look just like your dad,
And I agree,
'Yes, you are right,' I said.

After a hard day's work if he is sitting quietly
Or dozing in the armchair,
You can approach him with a problem, he will listen carefully,
He will say 'I care.'

My dad, (Ralph McIntosh), loves to sing and pray
Melodious tunes on his piano.
He plays every day,
I am happy that he taught my mother and I to play the piano.

As a cultivator he knows all about the soil
If there is a problem in my garden,
There is one person to call,
That is my dad, a very important man.

My mother, (Vivia McIntosh), a very important woman, loves to cook,
She is very good.
Like a magician she goes to the kitchen, she does not use a cook book,
She knows a lot about good food.

She makes up many recipes
And very good they are,
Whatever she brings to the table tastes scrumptious
Well worth waiting for.

Olive May McIntosh-Stedman

Our Outside Loo

Up garden path we had to go
Come rain, wind and often snow.
Light a candle in a jam jar,
Always blowed out for we'd gone far.
Out back door all shivery and black
Nerves have gone and want to run back.
But up I go past Dad's greenhouse,
Bit of a scream, just saw a mouse.
Stand shaking at loo, for a minute or more,
Then plucked up the courage to slam the door.
Run back indoors where firelight flickers,
Crying, 'Too late Mum, I've wet my knickers!'

Reginald Kerrison

It's In The Book

It's in the book,
The stories of old,
The tales of gold,
And treasures that's rarely been seen,
Of slaves being sold,
By pirates so bold,
The tales unfold.

Of travels in ships,
On planes and trains,
And now more modern the car,
It's in the book.

The whole human race,
Takes journeys through space,
Calling at various planets,
Jousting with stars,
Ursa Major and Mars,
It's in the book.

Amy Kerrison

Lost Days With Nan And Grandad

Everywhere I go and
All the places I have been
What is it I have seen?
Children clutching nanny's hand
Little girls, boys laughing gaily
Holding onto lovely toys
But me, no such pleasures
No laughing, girl and boy
Both to me are treasures
I never can enjoy
The sand, the sun, the seaside
Donkey rides and sticky rocks
Spinning wheels, more donkey rides
Seashells, candyfloss and ice cream
And seaweed tangled in their toes
It may all come true one day
But already it's too late

You see my steps are slower now
And not as fast as theirs
No, I could not keep up with them today
But I'll keep them in my prayers
Who knows, they maybe answered
Then, oh what fun it all will be
There will be Benjamin and Hayley
Grandad and of course me

B Clark

Nine Till Late

A few of us are yawning
Dare say some are scorning
Nearing end of morning
Lunch time is in sight
Afternoons of plight
Work on into night

M D Bedford

SNUGGY HOLE

I am lucky, I have a cat, she's torty and white,
And a great delight
On every occasion I give her a pat, as I love her with all my might.
She has a snuggy hole behind my desk,
Where she curls up tight, it's out of the way and a little dark.
But for me, she makes my life so bright.
My cat has snuggly holes beside me in bed,
The sun shines on her fur, a lovely hue, what else could be so nice?
When she speaks to me with a delightful miaow.

My cat is my favourite friend, we belong, she is bright and full of life,
Torty and white with whiskers long, she's pert and fun and so alive.
She's clever, with eyes so aware, she cuddles up to me at night,
And 'flowers' from love and care.
Friends may come and often go and part,
Loyalty is not always there.
But my cat, with a loving heart, follows me everywhere.

All curled, white and patterned, black red and white,
A mass of gentle fur, gentle paw, but hidden claws.
She stretches out for communication, tummy turned aside.
Cat, you clean and wash, clean as space above the air,
Eyes shut, pink tongue working, like a slave,
Working over the fur, a pride of self.
Stretch, stretch, eyes shut amongst the greenery

Anna Parkhurst

The Holiday

Tickets bought, the passports checked,
Bags are packed, the farewells said;
The holiday starts with a glass of wine,
With hopes of good food and a sun that shines.

The airports crowded with people going far,
Queues at checking desks nearly reaching the door;
Bags are weighed the labels attached,
To the departure lounge we're going at last.

Seat numbers are called it's time to alight,
Everyone hopes for a smooth quiet flight;
Flight bags stored, seat belts fastened,
The captain speaks in a calm quiet fashion.

The passengers cheer full of relief,
As the plane lands on the runway beneath;
Families alight to the sun and the glare,
Two weeks exploring and tales to share.

The room is clean, but it has seen its day,
Overlooking the pool, lots of games to play;
The sun beds laid out in nice tidy rows,
The sound of laughter and conversation grows.

Time passes quickly, it's time to return,
It's easy to spot all those with sunburn;
It took all year to save up to have fun,
All to spend two weeks away in the sun.

Janet Gardner

THE QUEEN'S GOLDEN JUBILEE

A truly wonderful time
Such as this I have never seen in my lifetime
So emotional and uplifting
I thought my heart would burst
In the field of spectacular
A ceremonial
We surely must come first
The people's participation
Was a glorious sight to see
With representation of every race and colour
An experience I never thought I'd see
It proved that it is possible
To display in harmony side by side
If this could be done day by day
Our country could restore its pride.

J E Greig

Now Miracles Don't Happen Anymore

The bed where I was born
was the largest bed in the world
and it stood in the largest room.

On the left a side table
supported Christian thoughts.
On the right, a mahogany wardrobe
supported the ceiling.

At the foot of the bed a dressing table
exhibited my mother's portrait
as she tilted her head
and brushed and brushed her multitude of hair,
then bundled up the beautiful cascade
with zigzag hairpins.

The blind back of the mirror
faced crimson curtains,
and when they travelled by rail
to release the morning,
sunlight broke in fragments on the floor
and the wide window burgeoned
an April-green wood.

I absorbed the silent benediction
of country sounds.
I heard through hopeful singing
complaints of cartwheels.
The pasture trembled under mighty hooves.
Wesleyan rooks preached with sore throats
from clumsy pulpits on a heavenly hill.
And faraway below the stranded house
I saw white globes of blossom in the orchard
while still innocent of snow.

At night I watched the moon
scrutinise my tiny fingers
and snuffed it with a movement of my hand.

Now miracles don't happen any more.
But in my age of discovery
a new found land leapt out at every turn,
and in my feathered dreams
I entertained a galaxy of angels
because my mother knew them to be there.

Peter Gillott

A Friendship Lost

I find it difficult to comprehend,
Why all this time, you would pretend.
A friendship good, went to bad,
An explanation, I never had.
I've tried so hard, to make amends,
I now accept we're no longer friends.
I miss the laughter, and our talks,
And going on those morning walks.
This bad feeling, will not last,
What went wrong is in the past.
We'll be friends again; I'm sure one day,
Friends for good, with no dismay.

Haley Frisby

Debt

I'm heavily in debt,
I receive so many demands for money,
The actual number I forget,
They completely fill a room,
They are in an enormous pile.
To have any more debt,
I'm totally in denial.
They've taken the TV back,
And they've repossessed the car.
I've torn up all my credit cards,
To spend any money,
On that I've put a total bar.
They've disconnected the phone,
The only meal I have,
Is when I share my dog's bone.
I know the bailiffs are coming,
For them I shall have to wait,
To be declared bankrupt,
That will be my eventual fate.
Buy everything with cash,
This you must not forget.
Then you'll have no money worries,
Because you will not be in debt.

F C Pelton

Childish Stories

I remember on my mother's knee
the fairy tales she told
they have never left me through the years
I still recall them now I'm old.

She spoke of how a lovely maid
was enamoured with this frog
when it turned into a prince
to set her eyes agog.

He was clean-cut and so debonair
a shining regal knight
he asked the maid to accompany him
to the royal ball that night.

She told him she was very poor
and dresses she had none
he waved his sword and in a puff of smoke
there were dresses by the ton.

He asked her then to make her choice
she was thrilled with exultation
the dress she picked it pleased the prince
filling him with jubilation.

He said she was his princess now
and he would meet her at the dance
just then he turned back into a frog
had the maiden missed her chance.

Lachlan Taylor

SPIRIT OF CHRISTMAS

Christmastime, my favourite time,
but not for the parties, presents and wine.
My joys are more simple
less costly as well.
Carols by candlelight
trees all aglitter,
tiny young faces
all lit up by their smiles.
The true spirit of Christmas
can never be bought.
It comes from within us
deep in our hearts.

Zandra Collisson

I'M SORRY

(Dedicated to SR)

I'm sorry for not being able
to make the wrongs seem right.
I'm sorry for being too young
to help you win the fight.
I'm sorry for what you went through
and the hurt that you received.
I'm sorry I couldn't be there for you
in the times you had to grieve.

I'm sorry I couldn't stop you
from leaving out of sight.
I'm sorry I couldn't change your mind
though I tried with all my might.
I'm sorry it has to end this way
but the candle can burn no more.
Instead I have to say, 'Goodbye'
and close the chapter's door.

Maria Jenkinson

Two Friends We Are

Two friends we are,
Who know each other,
Who seek the truth in all we do,
Who thirst for knowledge.

Two friends we are,
Who look and stare into each other's eyes and glare
Looking behind the cracked facade
Way deep beyond where the soul is found
Not daring to share what we've unfolded
The hidden secrets, that we're eluded
For fear of being mistrusted
Then rejected.

Two friends we are,
Who care so much about each other
Has to consider, for a better future,
And thus passionately hiding each other's hurt
At trying to make brand new fresh starts.

So forward we go with such optimism
Searching and searching for friends
Like we are.

Glen Head

No Score

My friend was posting a letter,
I said, 'Do me a favour mate,
Just drop this letter in for me,
Otherwise it could be too late.'

The letter contained my pools entry,
For which my hopes ran high.
When Saturday came with the soccer results
I felt I needed to cry.

To cry with happiness I stress,
For I had a winning line,
The world I once knew exploded
Now I had hit the big time.

I called up my mate that evening
I hardly knew what to say,
But he quickly brought me back down to earth
And I'll never forget that day.

He said, 'Friend, I've got some sad news for you,
When I arrived home that night,
Your letter was still in my pocket,
Forgive me my oversight.'

Gordon Barnett

My Dearest Sis

Who cracks a joke a day
Always annoying in every possible way

The one who throws her books about
Giving the most silliest looks around

The one who is full of surprises
Obviously shows in her twinkling eyes

She cares a lot about her surroundings
But when she is at home she does a lot of pounding

Even though a lot goes on with her
I can't help loving her very much.

Niresha Umaichelvam (9)

My True Dream

Driving on a journey, I was on the wrong side of the road
Dreams can jumble up your thoughts, as in the night unfolds
It was such a night my journey took me to this certain place
That I would find a lady friend who's goodness I'd embrace.

I stop, look down, before me saxifrage, softer steps along the way
A beautiful garden design by love's splendour, of wonder to display
Smilingly this lady came forward, greeted me
Invited to explore the garden, it was her property.

Sweet peas, many colours but mostly lavender white and red
Lining the pathway hydrangeas with multicoloured heads
A lovely wall built of beautiful coloured stone
To explore this garden made in dreams I have never known.

Walking round the garden, I espied a post hole started in
Hard small shallow water hole nearly to the brim
Although I was disabled my conscience I would help somehow
I made a promise to myself, I made a silent vow.

With now three friends joining us the lady invited me
To stay awhile, shepherd's pie, hot pot and a cup of tea
She handed me the cup, I notice with dismay
A crack and piece missing from the top, now in the saucer lay.

The lady vanished for a time, but in her absence to please her so
I would write a poem for her called 'spirit of the waters flow'
I knew I would be invited back at some future day
Then I knew what I must do, buy some more cups on the way.

Albert King

Can't Get It Right

I say my prayers every night,
But never seem to get it right,
I pray that we learn to tolerate,
Not have a world so full of hate,
And nobody need to be poor,
Then countries wouldn't have to go to war,
People could walk out safely at night,
Young people wouldn't want to fight,
Perhaps we could all learn to smile,
Be nice to each other, go that extra mile,
Children could go out to play,
Without the fear of being taken away,
Causing their families such needless pain,
When they don't come home again.
I wish some of my prayers could come true,
I don't think it's asking too much, do you?

Maureen Arnold

The Tree

There's a tree in my friend next door's garden with
branches reaching high,
Like an almighty giant reaching for the sky,
It's been there now for many a year, will remain long after we're gone
All through the days of summer I hear the birds in song
As they hop among the leaves they entertain us all
Throughout the days of summer till autumn leaves do fall.
Autumn sequel,
The mighty tree has gone now,
Rocking about in winds and rain, it became unstable
The surgeon came to see, if he could save the tree, alas he was unable
The chainsaw cut each twig and branch, finally the mighty trunk.

Gwendoline M Button

Retribution

Poor puss squatting on a ledge
Watched a sparrow on a hedge.
'I'm having that for tea,' he said,
And then rolled over - feigning dead.
But the sparrow with a twinkling eye
Said, 'He don't fool me - that stupid guy.'
And then he flew off low and swift
And dropped on puss his parting gift.

V B D'Wit

Shane My Friend

I had a lovely gift on Valentine's Day
A wee small pup from husband James.
Soft, dark velvet eyes, enough to melt your heart
It was a present, before we had to part.
Of course it couldn't replace dear husband James
But my pain diminished, as I got to know Shane.

Shane knew the time for his morning walk
His expression conveyed, *if only I could talk.*
He would take his lead down, and wait by the door,
Hurry up Mum, can't wait much more.

If next the neighbour's cat sat on our wall
Shane's look was of utter disdain,
Get off my wall you intruder
This is my territory, my domain.

Shane enjoyed his walk, explored every tree and flower
Happy years together, took away lonely hours.
He felt his duty was to look after me,
Especially chasing moggies up a tree,
Wonderful character, who felt his job so immense,
Barking at anything, moving - the other side of the fence,
The years rolled by, and a little weary was my friend,
I knew his life, was coming to an end
He managed a little wag of the tail,
And despite loving care, everything failed.
Shane is in that heaven for faithful friends,
But it isn't all sadness, or indeed the end.
A letter from James, to me was penned
Meet me at Bridgewater, from the train the nine ten,
James had returned to love me again.

S Palmer

THINKING OF YOU

My waking thoughts are of you, my love,
They entirely fill my heart.
I will always feel this way,
Together or apart.

You're on my mind the whole day long,
No matter what I do.
Wherever I am, or whom I'm with,
My thoughts are still with you.

As I fall into peaceful sleep
You linger through my mind.
You lull me to my rest, my sweet,
And still closer to me, bind.

David Mears

INSIGHT

There's a dragon to slay before breakfast
And another to fight before tea
Plus mountains to climb and rivers to cross
If I'm ever to find the real me.

For life is one continuous challenge
From the day you are born till you die
How you tackle each problem is vital -
Do you triumph or sit down and cry?

My pathway shows evidence of failure
- Less signs of victory than retreat -
But every night I vow to do better
So God will not say 'Who?' when we meet?

Betty Nevell

WATER WAYS

Sitting on a towpath watching a cat tease a rat.
Near the canal filled with rain
(Which was more than a drain).
I remembered my great, great grandparents,
They lived in this lane of water,
I'm the product of their daughter.
Born up the cut on a barge not very large,
Born on Tuesday gone on Wednesday.
Avoiding the local midwife's charge for delivery.
A horse called Bill, a teapot, a flower pot and pot to . . .
A cat (rat catcher) called King Harold
With just one eye couldn't catch a fly;
Them's your Brummies, eels in their tummies,
Yo can't tell me no different.

Vann Scytere

FUNNY

It's funny
It's true
I really do love you
You're a happy bird
That sings
You're the colour of the wind
You're the sweet, sweet sun
That shines
In this old heart of mine.

Helen Owen

MY VERY BEST FRIEND

(Dedicated to Frank Ajoku Jnr)

A friendship so special
A bond that we share
We'll always have each other
To listen and care

We talk for hours
Our pasts revealed
Between the two of us
Our secrets are concealed

Whatever we may need
Be it a favour or an ear
We always know
That the other is near

Our words are honest
From the heart, sincere
We can reveal all
We have nothing to fear

We'll always be friends
And get on well together
Not only now
In the future, forever

We'll always have support
And a shoulder to lend
You will always be
My very best friend.

Nathalie El-Korashy

My Dream

I'd love to be an author or a poet of renown;
I'd love to leave my mark, to show I've been around.
But I'm no good at English and at spelling I'm a clown;
But it doesn't stop me trying to win a golden crown!

I scribble down my verses, my writing's not much good;
I never was opinionated, my faults are understood.
I might just underestimate the brainbox I was given
And find that I am famous when I've gone to Heaven!

Hetty Launchbury

I Wonder If You Knew?

When I am old and I look back and
Start to reminisce
On all the wondrous things in life
That I happened to miss.
They'll make me sad I'm sure of that
But at least I'll know I knew.
Someone who was wonderful,
Who happens to be you.

Alan Garbutt

All Grown Up

'I want to go on again!' she cried,
'on the roller coaster or that big slide
that gets you ever so wet through . . .'
    'That will not be pleasant for you
    when we're in the car in that traffic jam.'
'I'm going on! I really am!'
    He said, 'It really is time we went,
    it's getting dark, our money's spent.
    We've been on every single ride,
    sometimes twice - be satisfied.'
'But we didn't have two goes
on that pirate ship.'
    'That made you queasy
    just looking at it!'
'I'm ready to try it
there isn't a queue.'
    'It's because they are closing
    and we shouldn't argue.
    We'll come again another time,
    on a holiday when the weather's fine.
    Do it all over - that's a cert!'
She sighed, 'Tomorrow
I am back at work.
It won't at all be this much fun.'
    He squeezed her hand,
    'I love you Mum.'

Angela Rawsthorne

(Sweep) Shadow

Months after Sweep died, the search began
To locate a rare Blue-Roan and tan.
I couldn't; so came Blue-Roan number three.
(Sweep) Shadow was what her name would be.

We needed to fill the empty space
With another Cocker's friendly face.
Some may think that one dog should do,
But one's only half as good as two.

Of course she's delightful as puppies are,
And our own special scintillating star,
Who seems to have a clever streak,
Learning her name within one week.

Biting feet is her main misdemeanour,
Affording her a great deal of pleasure.
A firm 'no' from me and she answered back,
So I had to use a different tack.

A whistle brought a positive result,
So I don't think it'll be too difficult
To get her to conform to what we desire,
Just consistency and patience we'll require.

Ina J Harrington

DEAR DIARY

Dear Diary,
    I told her today
Although I never really knew what to say
I had wanted to say it for a long, long time.
I didn't know how to say it, so I put it into a rhyme:
'Mum, I have been meaning to say this more and more.
No, don't look like that, I haven't broke the law
I wanted to say I appreciate the things you've done
I know half of them probably weren't fun.
You've always been concerned and worried about me.
It's like I'm in your brain, you've locked it and thrown away the key.
You've always been there when I've needed you
And you've always helped me too.
I can't thank you enough for what you've done,
I can keep on writing thank you again and again,
But soon I'm going to run out of pens.
So thank you Mum for all the things you've done.
You are the greatest under the sun!
So that's what I told my mum while she was doing the mop
And now I'm going to stop writing, otherwise my brain's going to *pop!'*

Anjolie Dhillon (12)

BAN ON PLAYGROUND GAMES

Imagine no more daisy chains
No ball games in the sun
No skipping ropes, no conkers -
What shall we do for fun?

How shall we use our energy?
Are we allowed to walk?
Or do we air our vocal chords
And merely shout or talk?

Will playgrounds become obsolete?
Will football disappear?
The world is changing swiftly
And childhood's gone I fear.

Health experts often tell us
That we really must be fit
And exercise our bodies
And not just daily sit.

But will kids deprived of outlets
For energy so great
Retain good health when older
And approaching Peter's gate?

Eileen M Pratt

The Bell's Toll
VE Day

(Cesena, Italy)

The bushy trees, the laden vines
By roadside, white and whirling dust.
The bulging grape - the ripen sign
For picking, near the chalky crust.
A village small - a church; the
Sign of cross, towers in the sky,
The roughen bricks with age and time,
The tolling bell - the echoing cry.

Ring, oh ring, Cathedral bells,
Lift up thy voice o'er Britain's land,
Shout loud the news your ringing tells
Of victory, that by the hand
Of God, was delivered to us
To guard, to treasure; and reap
The future with love and trust,
That never again shall women weep.

Chime out, oh bells of freedom,
Soar high upon thy wing to other lands,
Where free men long to join and sing
With us, the victory freedom song.
Ring out, ring out, oh Cathedral bells
Ring loud and clear, to warriors
Brave across the sea,
Your message for them tells of faith,
Good cheer, and certain victory.

Ernest Peaford

The Lady And The Lamp

The battles rage, the soldiers fight,
But way up yonder shines a light.
For the injured and dying she has come,
To tend the wounds of father and son.

Who is this woman with an angel's face
Tenderly caring and full of grace?
To the dying she whispers soft and low,
'Don't be afraid to let go.

There's a beautiful place just up ahead,
Where you can lay your weary head.
The sky is blue and the grass is green,
It's the most wonderful place you have ever seen.

Just close your eyes and you'll be there,
And I will say a little prayer.
I'll ask for God to give you His love,
Then He'll take you with Him up above.'

Now back to the wounded she has to go,
To tend to their wounds and to let them know.
She will not leave them in this strange land,
She will give them a helping hand.

With words so tender and eyes full of love,
Her hands are soft and white as a dove.
Who is this woman who walks round our camp?
Florence Nightingale, the lady with the lamp.

Margaret Anne Hedley

FRIENDSHIP

Friendship is something we can't do without
whatever happens to us we don't doubt
Lots of friendships give us pleasure
it can help us in our leisure.

One can be lonely without friends anyway
it makes one dreamy every day
Friends stand by us, whatever we do
that I am sure is always true

If we are not well, a friend we will tell
and they will come to see you until you are well
You don't need a doctor if it's not very bad anyway
and the friend will come to see you every day

Some of our friendships started long ago anyway
they went to school with us every day
We still keep in touch with them anyway
even if sometimes it's years until we see them one day

Some have gone abroad to live anyway
we certainly miss them every day
We keep in touch by letters anyway
we must not forget to do this anyway

Then there is a friend who lives near you anyway
she comes to see you nearly every day
And if we are not as we should be one day
she will make a point of calling anyway

Then there's my daughter-in-law who is my friend
she will help us all she could
If we are in need of help anyway
she will help us every day anyway

Yes friendship is something we all need
it's something we must do to others as well
Yes friendship certainly helps us no end every time
so we must not forget anytime

Then there is God in Heaven above
He's the one who gives us his love
so as love and friendships are really there any way
we must be friends to God every day.

Kay Taylor

FLOODS

Water, water, everywhere,
People stop to look and stare,
As the rains came pouring down,
The water rose upon the ground,
Houses were flooded,
People got scared, and none could say,
How much rain would fall on this day,
As people began to panic and despair,
You could hear a woman cry,
'Please save us from this terrible flood,
I think we are going to die.'

The ambulance crew and firemen came,
They gave the people hope,
Everyone felt safe once more,
They knew that they would cope,
People would survive,
As the rain began to stop,
The floods they began to subside,
People felt so lucky,
Just glad to be alive.

V M Ibbotson

My Friend, Jennie

A year has passed
Since we said goodbye
Jennie, Mondays aren't the same
Every week you always came.

Everyone knew your market stall
Full of haberdashery things
Cottons, materials, silks, needles etc.
What joy it used to bring.

I loved to hear about Cardiff
After you, Peter visited Clare
How hard it must be
With you no longer there.

The unconditional support you gave
To family, neighbours, friends
The pride you took with your garden
The pots, flowers, you did tend.

Immaculate to the end
You hair never out of place
You loved to shop with Viv
I picture the smile upon your face.

I miss the laughs we used to have
Always a lady to the end
A wonderful kind person
I was proud to call my friend.

Diana H Cramp

REFLECTIONS

Thistledown
And blackberries
Plums
And elder too,
Early signs
Of Autumn
Showing Summer
Is nearly
Through.
Spiders' webs
A'shimmering
With early morning
Dew.
Falling leaves,
All colours,
Ev'ry shade
And hue.
Thick mist
Upon
The river;
Fields hidden
From view;
This quiet
And thoughtful
Season
Showing
Nature
As true
As true.

Lyn Sandford

THE SPANISH DONKEY

There was once a donkey called Peppi,
Who lived on a farm, with no name!
He neighed and he brayed but to no avail,
Because nobody could understand what he said!

Poor Peppi was foreign,
Of that, he had no doubt.
His mates on the farm didn't like him,
Because he spoke with a foreign tongue!

He went about looking miserable
So sad, he could almost cry.
Nobody could talk or play with him,
No matter how much he tried.

Until, one day in summer,
His mate, the pony, took charge.
He taught him to speak English,
Which made him feel so proud!

He finished up feeling happy.
Giving rides, to small kids, on the sand.
He rarely spoke any Spanish,
But spoke English instead.

His story ended happily,
Because now he had loads of friends.
In fact, his mates, were proud to call him,
The best donkey they ever had!

Mary-Magdalene Kiddie

My Life

My life is more than halfway over,
Now I have reached 51.
I have eight children in my life.
My granddaughters and grandsons.

I also have my partner,
Whom I know I could not do without.
She is the one that has been there for me,
That there is no doubt

I know I have made mistakes in my life,
But I have tried my best.
I only care for the people I love,
So I don't worry much about the rest.

And my life I know for sure,
Will come to an end one day.
All my loved ones will be sad
But my enemies will shout hooray.

John Barr

The State We're In

Locked up
Like a bird in a cage
I need to express
My feelings of rage

Judges and lawyers
And those that seek power
Are corrupt as the day
And corrupt by the hour

Justice is sought
But often it fails
When innocent people
Are imprisoned in jails

The tabloids seek stories
Of sleaze and taboo
And much of their print
Is nothing but poo
They like stories they can run with for weeks
Anything's worthy if it sells their broadsheets.

Mark Tann

THE GREEN EARTH

A long time ago I was dressed in green with blue seas all around
My trees and grass were a sight to be seen, green covered all
of my ground
Mighty rivers flowed from my hills to the sea, trees grew in
great profusion
Then along came *Man* with his big ideas, to start all the confusion.

Where once magnificent forests grew they have planted concrete roads
Less trees to make the air smell clean, destroying wildlife abodes
My lovely rivers have now been dammed to harness all their power
Flooding vast areas of my land, killing plant and flower.

The air pollution *Man* has caused destroys so many things
The waste that's dumped on land and sea, destruction all around brings
Great cities grew as *Man* progressed. The millions must be fed
Whatever it may cost the Earth - just bleed me till I'm dead!

My lovely ozone layer is torn allowing harmful rays
To cause such damage everywhere, protection gone away
There was a cure for everything when first I came to be
But *Man* has lost a lot of that each time he felled a tree.

When I look down around the world at places which are barren
There's hunger, poverty, disease and death through *Man's* great harm
Floods, one place, drought another, nothing now as it should be
And who's to blame for all of this? It's *Man*, my friend - not me.

There must be something *Man* can do to stop this mass destruction
Or I, the Earth may destroy him with flooding and eruption
And in the end who wins? Not I, so we must work together
So that *Man* and Earth survive for now and then, forever.

Fran Thomson

You And I

If the future holds for me
Nothing more that I can see
I will let you know.

If the future takes away
All the things that once held sway
I will let you know.

If I can tell at all
That a world of spirits holds us all in thrall
I will let you know.

There is so much there
Of which to become aware.
If there is hope at all
I will let you know.

If there is anything
Left to do
Do it now before you die.
Just in case we don't come back
You and I.

Gladys Brunell

It's A Girl

Finally! She lets her eyelids drop. Is she asleep?
My heart it jumps, my knees too weak.
She cried for hours, bawled and crawled
My angel sleeps and I feel like a freak
Is it a whimper or a sigh?
If rest won't come, I'll surely die.

Did we know what we were doing?
Our only thoughts of smiles and cooing.
Four months on and she's still howling!
Mammy zombie-like! Daddy is scowling
Does reproduction enhance our vanity
Or could it be put down

To temporary insanity?

Mary O'Flynn

Poem Of Love

A poet of love
We see each day
Even in our work and play
We'll be together until the end
Yes my love you are my friend.

Each day I write this poem for you
Because my love you will be true
In the end that's what I'll do
I write this poem just for you.

My love for you
I'll never know
In my heart I'll love you so.

N Steven

HATRED

It eats away at your soul,
Your heart and your mind,
It makes inner peace,
Harder to find.

It tears you up,
And causes pain,
It takes over your life
And makes you insane.

Hatred is a feeling,
We could do without,
After all peace and goodwill
Are what life is about.

So start off small,
With family and friends,
Show a little more love,
And reverence.

Then extend to the world,
Show people you care,
We'll unite together
And stop hatred everywhere.

Ciara McBrien (16)

TUNA EYES

Don't give me those tuna eyes:
The half-closed lids, that indifferent stare.
Don't you think I know all your ruses by now,
The tone of your mews, your indifferent glare?
Don't give me that cute little wriggle -
It may make me giggle but *not* open a tin!

No use either slithering in and out of my legs,
You purry, furry ball now grinning.
No, not this time, not after yesterday's sinning:
Clawing the couch, nibbling my flowers,
Yes, you, sitting there exerting your power,
All beautiful, soft, noble as the sphinx . . .
Oh for God's sake, where's the blinkin' tin?
All right already, I'm defeated: you win!

Pamela Bakker

Running

It seems -
　　　　The whole world's on the run
　　　　Running to, running from.

Blast of shell and offshore gun
Traps the scared and scarred
In the melée of war,
Factions fight for political power
Bleeding and bewildered
Hopeless groups hurry on -

The innocent, haunted faces
With no place to hide,
No one to trust anymore.
The many, left behind,
Trussed in body bags,
Breathed their last breath,
Caught in the agony of war.

Children scream, the elderly fall,
Bundles heavier, stomachs emptier,
Leaden legs move ever away and on
Till - the whine, the blast, the moans;
Then the petrifying quiet -
No need to run anymore.

Oh God, where are you?

J McPherson

Thank You

(This is about a stray dog I took in
nine years ago. He passed away in January)

Do not be sad when I have gone
I want to thank you for everything you have done,
I had no one to love me, no one to care, no one to hug me when
I was feeling scared
Then you came along and took me in when everything
through my eyes was looking quite dim.
I want to thank you for being so kind, it helped me leave the past behind
Thank you for your tender, loving care,
and for always being there
I've had a wonderful life since being with you
I had someone to snuggle up to on bleak winter nights
and somewhere safe and warm for the rest of my life.
I don't want to leave but it's time to go
I'm old now you see
Thank you for loving me,
Toby.

Fell asleep 1 January 2002

Gloria Whitehouse

Exit

I'll be glad when I'm out of here
The plumbing, so noisy and that constant beat
It often knocks me off my feet.
I'll be glad when I'm out of here
The food's tasteless, but I'm putting on weight
And in a small space like this, that's not very great.
I've got rising damp up to my bald head
And the heat makes me itch in places least said.
It's dark and gloomy and such a bore
If only I could find that flipping door.
I'll be glad when I'm out of here
For it's not much fun just sucking a
Thumb all alone in my mummy's tum.
I'll be glad when I'm out of here.

H J Mazza

May

True are the words,
Befitting *May*
Flowers in their summer dresses
Blown away.
Black, grey clouds, darken the day,
Gale-force winds, and torrential rain.
Summer seems so far away,
No mowing of grass growing
Thicker and thicker.
Hedges and trees look forlorn,
Birds stay at home snugly
Warm in their nests.
Where the weather's concerned,
The birds know best.
Sea white horses ride the waves,
Beating hard against the rocks.
Throwing wide their spray,
'Change not a clout
Until May is out.'
Is what you hear old folks say.

Doreen Petherick Cox

I NEVER . . .

I never told my cat I loved her,
Never just sat down and hugged her,
Never stroked her silky fur,
Or listened to her peaceful purr.
I wish that I could stroke her now,
Just sit down and tell her how,
I never did want her to die.
But when she did, it made me cry.

Caroline Foster (13)

Billy Bob

Billy Bob was known as the jolly handyman,
because he went to work always with a happy smile,
His merry wife would faithfully pack his lunch,
which consisted of cucumber sandwiches and fruit pies.

For Billy Bob needed lots of energy to survive,
For he was a man of many talents and virtues,
A master of all things twice,
For he always chased away the mice.

He was a carpenter by trade,
But many knew him as a plumber too,
An electrician, a plasterer, a roofer they knew,
A road man and a ganger, just to mention but a few.

The tools he used were numerous and many,
Some he stowed behind the loo,
There were screwdrivers and assorted hammers,
Different saws and chisels, nails, tacks and pins,

Pliers, grips and planes, ring spanners and open ones,
Blowtorches and soldier, bends and springs,
Wire-cutters and fuses, lamps and metal rings,
Trowels and spirit levels to help you sing.

Plus he used his elbows a lot with good old grease,
Assorted woods and tiles, felt and itchy lagging,
String-lines and paving stones,
Because everything would have to be level.

But Billy Bob did not always come home very jolly
Because most of the time he was very tired,
But even so, he always wore a smile,
For his pretty endearing wife was named Pretty Polly.

Billy Bob, was known as the jolly handyman,
because he went to work always with a happy smile.

James S Cameron

A Slug!

It's dark, warm and damp outside - down in the garden.
The lush fresh leaves and scented blooms are calling,
As I slither and slide out from my dark and safe hide
I leave my silvery cord smeared across the walling.

Now free, I stretch, reach and my form extending,
Dual antenna swirling high erect and waving.
The scented vegetation wafts upon the breeze,
I am careful, slow but handsomely appalling.

Gliding with effortless slight towards my intended target.
My blackness hides me as I gleam under a silvering moon.
My belly squirming coloured yellow and orange,
The shelled snails seeing me pass, all swoon.

Further and closer now to those succulent stems,
Freshest leaves waver and dance upon the air.
I make my way across dampened dark loam pens,
Apparently protecting the plantings so cared.

The first crunch and then the munch of my formless jaw,
Liquidised leaf matter slides in effortless grace.
Greening soup and chewed stemmed maw,
Digesting quickly as soon as it passes my face.

What's that I sense now upon the moving air?
An intoxicating aroma that passes my guards?
I move towards this attractive scented trail,
Down and across towards a part-filled pail.

Ahh, I sit and then I take a sip, of a strange and darkening brew.
My antenna swirls and then gets confused conjoined as a helix twirl.
My senses reeling now, not even knowing what's true,
My back and my sides are shivering now as I curl.

Dropping over the edge I plop into honeydew sweet liquor,
And I sup and I gulp and I feel so very fine
My senses drowning now quickly recede from such safe succour
So I fear no ill now as I depart - up to that place so divine - hic!

Michael Boase

When It's Dark

The journey home is a long one,
That is when it's dark.

Like swimming back to land,
When you're followed by a shark.

Going home in daylight seems really very short,
But going home at night you just want it to abort.

In the dark you dream of seeing the big hot sun
You blink once more to see the day has just begun.

Bex Jones

SCAMP

Now there was this dog who had a bone
but what he wanted was a home.
He was a stray who roamed the streets
lying in rubbish tips when he sleeps.
When he was hungry he would go to people's backyards,
pulling down the dustbins, looking for scraps, so as not to starve.
His coat was black and mangy, the life he did lead
a lead and new collar is what he did need.
Now on this day as he crossed a busy road
he was hit by a truck which carried a big load.
Lying there all bloody, the driver got out of his cab
and crying, the driver was really sad.
Picking up the dog he took him to a vet,
Saying 'Please patch him up, I'll be in your debt.'
Days went by, the dog was beginning to heal
A bond was forming, he began to feel.
Feeling sorry for the dog, he brought him home,
to live with his family and give him a bone.
They cleaned him up, no more like a tramp,
his two little children, they called him Scamp.
Scamp is now happy he has found a home,
new lead and collar and sometimes a bone.

N McManus

The Hopeless Gardener

The dandelion I spared last spring
Has thriven. I justified my pride
In its handsome head, saying
I would use the leaves for salad;
I used a few,
Then it became lost to view.
Today, to make some space
To put the potatoes in,
I find it again.
Brave plant, brave lion-head,
Handsome creature.
I shall never
Be a good gardener.
Something democratic in me stays the hand
That would deracinate, a feeling
Every plant has equal right
To make the best of itself, show what it can do,
That sow-thistle, last year,
Was tall and magnificent, the superb
Achievement of the life within it.
Nettles, because they sting,
Are my enemy,
But yet they are such a valiant company,
Never losing heart
However oft assaulted.
To dig them up seems mean.
Perhaps if I leave just a few
To grow again,
I shall remember when I see them young and green
That nettle tea is deemed a healthy brew.

Jean Overton Fuller

Wisdom And Truth

Secretly - as the light grows dim
The small folk that hide from the day,
Creep from their lair
And take to the wing,
To fly in the cool night air.
Where they sing the songs
Their ancestors sang.
In the days that have gone before.

Invisibly - as the stars appear,
They hover on outspread wing,
Their intricate dance
Is as old as time.
As old as the songs they sing,
And they dance the dance
Their ancestor's danced.
In the days that have gone before.

Soundlessly - the Earth whirls on,
While high in the wide night skies,
They perform the rites
Of wisdom and truth.
Things the world has forgot,
And the little folk wish
For the time-worn ways,
Of the days that have gone before.

Quietly - as the dawn breaks through,
They slip away, hand in hand,
Back to the shadows
That hide them away.
Far beneath the unknowing land,
And the small folk wait
For their time to come.
As it was in the days gone before.

Leonie Lewis Park

Carols

In the great cathedral spaces
Light with shadow interlaces.
Kings and queens in sculpted stone
Mark history for ever gone.

As the congregation rises
And the rolling sound comprises
Bass and alto notes which soar
To match the organ's mighty roar

Then, high above, a young voice sings
As pure and fresh as mountain springs
In descant carolling the air

Sung: 'Oh that we were there - ere!
Oh that we were there!'

Evelyn Westwood

TEEN-AGERS

In the past 18 years I've aged a 100,
Are my offspring's to blame, in the main?
No one warned me what I was in for,
The torment, anguish and ongoing pain . . .

The sleepless nights, ailments and 'Mummy?'
Mummy why, what, wherefore?' and more.
'Oh, leave me in peace, please I need rest!'
My sanity in question: 'Silence!' I implore.

At last! Off to school; some precious time alone!
Brain dead and exhausted I wonder where I'm at,
Depressed and deluded, I turn to comfort eating,
Clothes start to shrink; strong denial. I'm not fat!

Husband goes a wandering, in search of leaner fayre.
But I'm too engrossed to notice, school activities and such,
PTA events, brownies, cubs, just to mention a few.
Piano lessons, ballet. Oh, and clean the rabbit hutch.

'Come to the gym!' My fellow sufferers plead,
You won't be disappointed, the personal trainer's great!
So off I go in earnest, dreaming of chocolate pudding;
Is anybody listening? Please help me get things straight.

Prayers are partly answered, my offsprings now are teens.
I'm free to rejoin the human race, but I realise it's too late,
The spirit's willing, the flesh is worn out, and no one
Wants you when you're old, especially in this state.

And so the cycle carries on, the fledglings leave the nest
I hope they heed my words: study, focus, get a career.
Avoid what I've become: myopic, menopausal, out of touch.
Hey! Bartender I'm still waiting! What's happened to that beer?

Susan Murphy

A New Beginning

A new life had begun
On that chosen day
So special and so precious
In every single way

I will protect you from harm
I will shelter you from your fears
I am here little one
And I always will be near

There is no need for you to wish
Upon that faraway star
Because we all love you
Just the way that you are

So baby if you need me
Do not be frightened just to say
My first ever little cousin
Who we were blessed with on that day

Hayley Vernon

TEMPTATION

Many promises made to resist, the chocolate temptation
Of savouring the delights of a wonderful creation
The smooth silky flavour an untold elation,
A joy to revel, in forbidden jubilation.

Those clever confections to tempt us all
In artistic wrappers, large or small
When the fancy takes us, temptation calls
For that chocolate delight, what ever befalls.

Forget those warnings of expanding girth
Laugh at the revelation, and enjoy with mirth
That wonderful flavour, so smooth on the tongue
A positive delight enjoyed by every one.

What better answer, to relieve such stress
Than that forbidden most clever confection, no less
A quiet moment of exquisite delight
A trip to Heaven, with every bite.

C King

Joe

You were always there when I was down,
You never acted like a clown.
You always had a happy face,
You were such a case.

Travelling at your own pace,
You never won a race.
But who needs a winner,
When I had a friend like you?

A few years went by,
You looked unhappy, I don't know why?
I found out you were 24,
And soon you would be at death's door.

A few days later, the news came,
You left my heart in great pain.
Every day I think of you,
My faithful horse, I will miss you.

Alice Isaac (12)

Grown Up

G rown-up's are a pain
R ound the bend, they drive you insane
O n and on about don't do this, don't do that
W orn out by the time they finish, how boring is that?
N ag, nag, nag, that's all they do.

U p to only telling you off, for doing something wrong
P ush off parents, you've been at it too long.

Yvonne Hopkins

My Girls

Emma came first, by no means the worst.
Small and slightly dumpy.
Then along came Clare, my what a girl,
But for mornings, unfortunately grumpy.
My trio, yes three, our Jo hit the scene,
All legs and arms - very charming,
But the whirlwind arrived, four in the gang,
Bronagh, everyone's darling.

Well I taught them to walk
And eventually talk.
And never a moment, a dull one.
My purse never large,
Was increasingly charged
For the activities they do,
And they have some.

Would you swap for my boys?
My friends would implore.
On occasion, the thought crossed my mind.
But if you had my girls,
Yes, my beautiful pearls,
I assure you the offer won't stand.

And you know through the years,
Most happy, some tears.
To exceptional women they've grown.
And, I never will find, such contentment of mind,
Than I have from the seeds that I've sewn.

Theresa McVeigh

BIG KIDS ON KIDS

A mum of three
'Are you talking to me?
I'm busy doing the dinner.
Take off that uniform, stick it in the machine,
Want to hurry, get all those things clean.'

No time on my own, all I do is moan
'Quick get up it's eight,
Better not get into school late!
Is your homework done?'
I eat on the run.

'Polish those shoes and brush those teeth right,
Come and read, I haven't got all night.
Don't step in that puddle, time for a cuddle,
Clean up those toys.'
Oh, the joys of my boys

Tara Harvey

Boys

He arrives in the world with great impact
Your heart just swells with pride
You sort the nappies, burps and sick
And set your life aside.

After great encouragement, his first steps come
And you wipe away a tear.
But soon the video's filled with jam
And the poor cat shakes in fear.

First day at school - a welcome thought:
Smart uniform, nice clean shirt
Bit different later - ruffled hair,
Grazed knee, and smeared in dirt.

You watch as he scores, playing football
Jump up and scream on the line
His friends laugh and sneer 'Who's mother is *that!'*
He replies 'I dunno - she ain't mine.'

He does well at school, and lands a good job
But still comes home for his tea,
One day he meets the girl of his dreams,
They marry, and soon they are three.

So once again you hold a babe
That fills your soul with joy
And you see that familiar look of pride
In the eyes of your lovely boy.

Pam Samways

THEN AND NOW

I look out on the horizon
what do I see?
I see beauty and wonderment
who made this all for me?
I smell this strange aroma
what could it be?
It's flowers, grass and trees
every scent so special to me.
I hear the sweetest sounds
what can they be?
The sounds of baby lambs
and birds in the tree.

Am I still asleep and dreaming
or could I be remembering?
The air was once so pure
the sky the clearest blue,
grass reflected morning dew
oceans, rivers of the finest hue,
things lived and grew as they should
not just for us as food,
when and where did we humans
go so *wrong?*

Christine Anne Davies

Beetle's Tale

There once was a rusty and battered old car
Worn out, because he had travelled so far.
Today he's unhappy, he couldn't feel bluer.
His owners have changed him for one that is newer.

He knows that he doesn't look 'posh' any more.
His headlight is smashed, there's a dint in his door.
His tyre is punctured and he's not too reliable.
To keep him wouldn't be economically viable.

The model he's next to is shiny and bright.
He wished that he could just get out of sight.
When folk come to look, him they'll not want to buy.
It's his neighbour, 'Sam Speedy' who'll catch everyone's eye.

Next day something happens, in comes a young chap
And he calls to the owner 'I'm looking for scrap'
The boss of the garage who's name's Frederick Creeple
said 'Come over here then and look at this Beetle.'

The young chap said 'Marvellous!' and jumped up in glee!
'He's just what I want.' Fred said 'Take him, he's free.'
So later that day, along comes Albert Taylor,
And loads the old Beetle up on his long trailer.

'They may not have wanted you mate, but I do
By the time I have done, you'll be shiny and new.
I'll tune up your engine, spray paint on your body,
Within a few days, you'll no longer be shoddy!'

Albert works on the Beetle and it soon looks brand new.
Fresh headlights, engine turned, and painted bright blue.
Said Albert. 'You're lovely, you were worth all the fuss.
And God feels the same about each of us!'

Daphne Askew

THE LOUD AWAKENING

Up woke Michael in his mistress's bed
His eyes bulged out at the sight of the bedspread
For there before his very eyes
Was a monster of some awesome size
It jumped up and down on Michael's feet
His legs felt like lead up to his thighs I might repeat
Michael's heart it did pound
His eyes flicked around
When suddenly to his dismay
The creature shouted 'Come and play'
At that point Isabelle his mistress
Walked in with his breakfast, having no thought of distress
She said 'Give you a fright darling did my male robot?
I hid him away, but I forgot
To shut the kitchen door whilst I made your breakfast
He is so agile, quick and mighty fast
Stairs are no problem, he loves to get around
Jump off the bed, you troublesome hound.'
A mighty laugh came from his body
And off he jumped and sidled on his doddy
Michael, wide-eyed shook with fear
Isabelle unladened herself of the breakfast gear
Jumped into bed with Michael still in a stupor
But, once in Isabelle's arms, her odour
Of roses scent put Michael no longer in despair
Let us leave them, once more a loving happy pair

Alma Montgomery Frank

WHICH ONE OF YOU

Which one of you do I like
Which one will I hate
If I try the wrong one
Will it be a mistake?

Which one of you do I like
Which one do I hate
Which one should I go out with
Who will get me home, not too late?

Which one of you do I like
Which one do I hate
Oh which one should I marry
Before it is too late?

Keith L Powell

I Had A Dream

I am not so young now,
So many changes I have seen,
Like the concrete grey of motorways,
Replacing fields of green.

Years ago you could travel,
Not far from a smoky town,
To see fields, forests and rivers,
Nature wearing her crown.

Now the journey it takes longer,
Boring motorways everywhere,
No scenery to look at,
Just road and bridges there.

Oh to replace road with green grass,
Car horns with sweet bird songs
Then perhaps we can put,
Nature's crown back where it belongs.

Jean Stratford

It Must Be Very Hard For Trees

It must be very hard for trees
to carry the snow on their back
and have the wind laugh at them
tickling their leaves.
It must be very hard for trees
to stand so still and watch
the birds fly high into the sky.

It must be very hard for trees
not to talk when they have
so many stories to tell.

The other day though, I thought
I saw one smile when a little child
hugged it and kept
standing there saying ‘Happy tree!’

To him the tree was God.

Marion Schoeberlein